Understanding
AFGHANISTAN
Today

WITHDRAWN

Don Nardo

AFGHANISTAN

Mitchell Lane
PUBLISHERS
P.O. Box 196
Hockessin, Delaware 19707

A Kid's Guide to
THE MIDDLE EAST

Understanding Afghanistan Today

Understanding Iran Today

Understanding Iraq Today

Understanding Israel Today

Understanding Jordan Today

Understanding Lebanon Today

Understanding Palestine Today

Understanding Saudi Arabia Today

Understanding Syria Today

Understanding Turkey Today

Andkhvoy
Aqcheh
Balkh
Mazar-e Sharif
Kholm
Kondoz
Talogan
Feyzabad
Bahōrak
Langar
Sheberghan
Balkh
Konduz
Takhar
Badakhshan
Faryab
Meymaneh
Tokzar
Samangan
Baghlan
Skazar
Warsaj
Bala Moraḥab
Geysar
Belcheragh
Jowzjan
Samangan
Baghlan
Kushka
Badghis
Dowshi
Kapisa
Konar
Towraghondi
Koshkekohneh
Sayghan
Bamian
Chaghcharan
Ghōrband
Dowlat Yar
Penjab
Kowt-e Ashrow
Charikar
Raqi
Laghman
Mehtarlam
Asadabad
Jalalabad
Karokh
Gal'eh-ye Now
Bamian
Parvan
Rowzanak
Herat
Shahrak
Garghareh
Kabul
Herat
Ghowr
Teywarah
Afghanistan
Ghazni
Vardak
Lowgar
Nangarhar
Parachinar
Shindand
Ghazni
Baraki
Gardeyz
Paktia
Anar Darreh
Oruzgan
Mushaki
Zareh Sharan
Badam Mazar
Tarin Kowt
Shab Juy
Farah
Farah
Khash
Delaram
Shorawak
Paktika
Lash-e-Joveyn
Lashkar Gah
Sinjri
Zabol
Galat
Jaldak
Darwazgai
Khash
Gandahar
Zaranj
Hauz Qala
Nimruz
Helmand
Kandahar
Gal'eh-ye Fath
Deshu
Khannan
Pulalak
Gowd-e-Zereh

TURKEY

SYRIA

LEBANON
IRAQ

PALESTINE

ISRAEL
JORDAN

IRAN

AFGHANISTAN

SAUDI
ARABIA

Mitchell Lane
PUBLISHERS

Printing   1   2   3   4   5   6   7   8   9

Library of Congress Cataloging-in-Publication Data
Nardo, Don, 1947–
 Understanding Afghanistan today / by Don Nardo.
     pages cm. — (A kid's guide to the Middle East)
 Includes bibliographical references and index.
 ISBN 978-1-61228-652-5 (library bound)
 1. Afghanistan—Juvenile literature. I. Title.
 DS351.5.N37 2014
 958.1—dc23
                                                                                    2014013221
eBook ISBN: 9781612286754

PUBLISHER'S NOTE: The narrative used in portions of this book are an aid to comprehension. This narrative is based on the author's extensive research as to what actually occurs in a child's life in Afghanistan. It is subject to interpretation and might not be indicative of every child's life in Afghanistan. It is representative of some children and is based on research the author believes to be accurate. Documentation of such research is contained on pp. 60–61.

The Internet sites referenced herein were active as of the publication date. Due to the fleeting nature of some web sites, we cannot guarantee they will all be active when you are reading this book.

To reflect current usage, we have chosen to use the secular era designations BCE ("before the common era") and CE ("of the common era") instead of the traditional designations BC ("before Christ") and AD (*anno Domini,* "in the year of the Lord").

PBP

CONTENTS

Introduction: They Will Bounce Back 6

CHAPTER 1: A Day in Mustala's Life 9
    Problems Posed by Gender.............................13

CHAPTER 2: Natural Physical Features......................15
    A National Treasure and Hero of the Struggle 19

CHAPTER 3: A Giant Battlefield...............................21
    Widely Viewed as Barbaric 27

CHAPTER 4: Diverse Peoples Seek Unity 29
    Who Are the Nuristanis?................................33

CHAPTER 5: Families, Women, and Children 35
    Bartered Daughters 41

CHAPTER 6: Religion as a Way of Life......................43
    The Famous Blue Mosque...............................47

CHAPTER 7: Literature, Arts, and Entertainment......49
    "I'll Never Return" 53

Afghanistan Recipe: Kabeli Pilau 54
Afghanistan Craft: Paper Hamsa..........................55
What You Should Know About Afghanistan..............56
Timeline 57
Chapter Notes 58
Further Reading 60
Glossary...62
Index 63

BOLD words in text can be found in the Glossary

Introduction

"I love my country," said Meena Keshwar Kamal, a poet and promoter of women's rights, in a poem she wrote in 1980 to honor her native land of Afghanistan. It is the easternmost nation of the Middle East, which stretches more than 2,000 miles (3,200 kilometers) westward to Egypt and encompasses 14 countries. One of the primary reasons for her affection toward Afghanistan is "its towering mountains." Afghanistan's many rugged peaks have sometimes discouraged foreign conquerors. They had "risen to stand against the intruders."[1]

However, some of those intruders invaded Afghanistan. The result of those invasions has been a long series of terrible wars. Each one ravaged the country, causing much death and

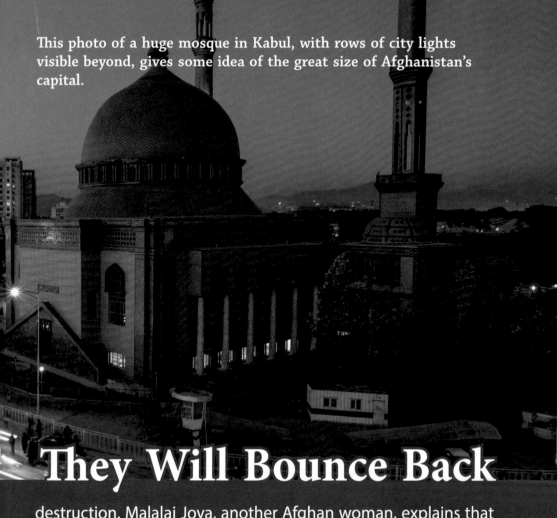

This photo of a huge mosque in Kabul, with rows of city lights visible beyond, gives some idea of the great size of Afghanistan's capital.

They Will Bounce Back

destruction. Malalai Joya, another Afghan woman, explains that "my country has suffered." There has been almost constant war, she adds, which caused much poverty. And "more than half of Afghan men and 80 percent of women are **illiterate**."[2] That means that they cannot read and write.

Yet Afghans have repeatedly shown themselves to be a tough, courageous people. They refuse to let centuries of adversity destroy them. In Meena Kamal's inspiring words, her countrymen and countrywomen "will never bow down [to] or obey" invaders. They will bounce back, "even after their villages

Two Afghan boys collect garbage, for which they will receive a small payment. That money will be used to help their poverty-stricken families. Many other children in Kabul polish shoes, clean cars, or do other menial tasks and rarely, if ever, have time to go to school.

CHAPTER 1
A Day in Mustala's Life

"I think Afghanistan could be a great country," says 13-year old Mustala. "If I was the president, I'd help all the poor people and make sure they have food and electric lights."[1]

Mustala mentions food and electric lights for a good reason. He often is hungry. And his house has no electricity. Mustala lives in Afghanistan's capital, Kabul, with his grandparents. "We are really poor," he explains. "My grandparents don't work. We have no money for soap, so I am often dirty and wearing dirty clothes."[2]

Mustala's parents are still alive. But as so often happens in Afghanistan, his family was torn apart during wartime. His father angered some men in his neighborhood and they threatened to kill him. So he fled to Iran, which borders Afghanistan on the west. Mustala was only three or four at the time. Several years later his mother married again. She and her new husband moved to another country, leaving Mustala with her parents. Mustala's voice is sad when he speaks about his mother. "Her new husband would not want me to live with him,"[3] he says.

Because his parents both left him behind, Mustala has a hard life. However, he is hardly alone in his plight. Nearly every child in his poverty-stricken neighborhood lives in much the same way. Most of the houses are made of **mud-bricks** or wooden poles covered by mud and typically have no more than two rooms. So there is little privacy.

One of Mustala's neighbors, 14-year-old Karima, has no privacy at all. She and her brother and three sisters live in her uncle's house. In all, more than 10 people share just one room. "There are not enough mats for us all to sleep on," she says. "So my family sleeps on the floor, a cold and hard place to sleep. The house has no electricity. When it becomes dark outside, it becomes dark inside. I have no way to do my homework."[4]

Mustala has the same problem. But he worries less about his homework than about having enough to eat. He gets up early each morning, eager to go to school. As he dresses, he is not thinking about the day's lessons. Instead, his mind is on his next meal. "I get free food at school," he explains. It "is often the only time I eat." And sometimes, "my grandparents don't eat at all. When I can, I put food in my pockets at lunchtime to take back to my grandparents. But it is a thing that makes me nervous to do. I don't want to get in trouble. So sometimes if I'm hungry for two pieces of bread, I take two. But I don't eat them. I hide them in my jacket to take home."[5]

Whether walking to school or back home, Mustala and his classmates face another problem. The air is frequently hard to breathe. Kabul is a **populous**, crowded city. The last time someone counted, in 2011, more three million people lived there. Many streets are not paved. So cars, trucks, and wagons throw up a lot of dust. "The streets are very dusty," Mustala's neighbor Sigrullah points out. "And lots of children become sick from the dust."[6]

When Mustala arrives at school, he tries to study hard. Sometimes he is distracted. Like many other schools in Afghanistan, there is little clean drinking water. And there are no toilets. Also, he does not know how long he will be able to go to school full-time. Poverty forces many Afghans his age to attend school part-time. They go two or three hours in the morning and then work the rest of the day. It helps their families make ends meet.

One such part-time student is 11-year-old Rhamat, who is in the fourth grade. "I go to school from ten in the morning until one" in the afternoon, he says. After that, "I work in my father's tailor shop or his food shop. When I finish school, I would like to be a mechanic, fixing cars and motorcycles."[7]

In fact, Rhamat hopes of someday owning his own mechanic's shop. Earnestly, he says, "I would like to show children from another country my shop." He also envisions taking them to the local marketplace. Most of all, he dreams of

Those Afghan children who do manage to attend school, either part or full time, often do not have desks or chairs. As seen in this photo, they do the best they can while sitting on the floor. They are usually very serious about learning, as evidenced by the look of deep concentration on the face of the nine-year-old boy in the foreground.

showing them Kabul's zoo. "My favorite animals," he says, "are the monkeys and a small cow. It would be nice to work at the zoo. I would feed the animals. I would especially like to take care of the cow."[8] Sadly, Rhamat will not be able to work at the zoo if he lacks the proper education. That means he needs to go to school full-time rather than part-time.

Meanwhile, Mustala hopes he can continue attending his own school full-time. He understands that school is very important for his future. Education is necessary "to make a good country out of Afghanistan," he declares. "Right now we are a **backwater** country."[9] It is not just poverty that makes his country less wealthy and successful than many others in the world, he says. It is also fear. At night, after a day of school and doing chores for his grandparents, he is tired. And he looks forward to a good night's sleep.

But Mustala and his friends are often awakened at night by gunshots and screams. Sometimes these sounds are far-off. At other times they are uncomfortably close. As a result, Mustala and many other Afghans feel that their streets are not safe. The dangers prevent them from doing all the things they feel will make them successful and happy. "It can get scary," Mustala almost whispers. "At school I have learned there are better ways to do things than all this war, war, war all the time." In a more hopeful tone, he makes a prediction. "It's the young generation that will change that!"[10]

PROBLEMS POSED BY GENDER

Not all Afghan children are as poor as Mustala and his neighbors. Some families are somewhat better off. They live in larger houses with three, four, or even more rooms. Yet they, too, often struggle to get a decent education.

Jeena, aged 16, is a case in point. Her gender poses certain problems, not only for schooling but also for having a job. This is because of strict social traditions pertaining to women. Many Afghan men think women should be sheltered at home. In this view, women's main role in society is having children and raising them, so education is pointless.

These Afghan girls are students at a high school in the small city of Bamiyan, lying about 149 miles (240 km) northwest of Kabul. Before 2002, girls in Afghanistan were not allowed to attend school.

At least, Jeena says, her own parents are "broad-minded." Most Afghan parents, she continues,

> marry off their daughters at fifteen or sixteen or seventeen years old. It is hard for girls here. If they work outside [the home], people say bad things. They say it is not good for a woman to go out. They should stay at home and be a housewife. Many girls say, "At fifteen or eighteen, we are going to be married. We don't need an education." But most girls do want an education. My friends want to study English and computers. . . . I go to an outside class for computers at six in the morning, before school. But my family won't let me go to outside classes that are **coed**. I can't go against the wishes of my family.[11]

Taken from an airplane, this photo shows the jagged, arid terrain of the Baba mountain range. Situated in eastern Afghanistan, these peaks are the western extension of the mighty Hindu Kush range that runs along the border with Pakistan. The rugged, barren, chaotic nature of this landscape explains in part why over the centuries so many invaders have found it difficult to capture and hold Afghanistan.

Natural Physical Features

According to a traditional **adage**, "Afghanistan is the graveyard of empires." The exact origins of the phrase are uncertain. Many scholars attribute it to Mahmud Tarzi (1865–1933), an early modern Afghan writer and thinker. Those proud words suggest that Afghanistan cannot be conquered. That is, no foreign invader has ever managed to completely overrun the country and control it.

However, a quick glance at Afghanistan's history shows that this adage is a myth. Over the course of many centuries, a number of outside powers did take over the country. Yet a grain of truth does lie in those words. First, all foreign foes discovered that gaining control of Afghanistan was exceedingly difficult. It required a great deal of time and effort. And it cost many lives. Also, even after taking the chief city, Kabul, administering the countryside proved complex and costly. Many such outsiders eventually decided Afghanistan was not worth the effort. So they left.

One reason intruders have long found Afghanistan a hard challenge is that its people are tough and defiant. An even more crucial factor is its **geography**, or natural physical features. Some of these features are so extreme that Afghans are challenged nearly as much as outsiders. First, the country's landscape is incredibly mountainous. Tall, jagged peaks cover three-quarters of the nation. The highest are in the massive Hindu Kush range. With several mountains taller than 20,000 feet (6,100 meters), the range dominates the country's central region. Hundreds of deep valleys alternate with towering snow-capped peaks. Traveling from one valley to another is often time-consuming and tiring. This has long proven a major obstacle to natives and outsiders alike.

Another barrier to foreign intruders is Afghanistan's unusually dry climate. Some fertile areas do exist among the mountain valleys and elsewhere. But there are relatively few lakes and rivers for such a large country. Moreover, three immense deserts cover the lowlands south of the central mountains. One is the Dasht-i Margo, or "Desert of Death." Rocky rather than sandy, it has claimed the lives of countless invaders who tried to cross it.

From freezing mountaintops to scorching deserts, Afghanistan is therefore a land of extremes. It is no wonder so many outsiders have found it uninviting and hard to manage. Monik Markus, an ambassador's assistant at Afghanistan's embassy in Washington, DC, describes the "rugged terrain and seasonally harsh climate." These "presented a challenge," she says, to "conquering armies for centuries."[1]

These realities show how Afghanistan's geography helped to shape its history and culture. Historian Shaista Wahab, born and raised in Kabul, explains another factor. Namely, the country rests in a **strategic**, or important and opportune, position. It is on a path that traders and armies often took in past ages. These, Wahab says, are "the ancient trade and military routes between East Asia and the Middle East."[2]

This special location made control of Afghanistan very tempting and useful to aggressive outsiders. Some foreign

---

IN CASE YOU WERE WONDERING

Are there useful or valuable minerals in the vast mountain chains?
Yes. Deposits of zinc, nickel, lead, copper, asbestos, sulfur, iron ore and mica have been discovered. Valuable gemstones such as amethysts, rubies, jade, and quartz are mined in some places.

armies needed to pass through it on the way to somewhere else. Others tried to conquer Afghanistan so they could dominate those overland routes. And still others invaded because their leaders wanted to control all of Asia. Thus, to many Afghans' regret, Wahab writes, they lived in "a crossroads of cultures."[3]

In the meantime, contact with foreign peoples affected the natives. Afghans could not avoid absorbing ideas, beliefs, and customs from each new group. For that reason, remnants of several of those cultures remain today. They can be seen, for example, in one of the national languages, Pashto. Many of its words came from the languages of past conquerors.

Not all of Afghanistan's natural features are nonliving. No less important to its people and culture are its **indigenous** plants and animals. At first glance, a stranger might think the country has no plants. This is because its huge stretches of rocky peaks are the first thing most visitors see. As a result, only about one percent of the land is forested.

Although those woodlands are small, they feature a wide range of tree types. Among them are spruce, larch, hemlock, pine, alder, juniper, willow, birch, oak, and ash. Also growing in the forests are numerous kinds of herbs. Afghan healers use several of them to treat illness. They include saffron, coriander, anise seed, and cumin, among others.

Most of the rest of Afghanistan's native plants take the form of crops. Local farmers raise them mainly in the valleys and a few small lowland areas. "Annual rainfall is low," Wahab points out. "Most farmlands are located near streams and rivers for easy access to irrigation water."[4]

The country's limited stores of fresh water also support its **fauna**. Some, like goats, sheep, and cattle, are kept as livestock. They supply meat, dairy products, and hides. The Afghans also

These women workers are separating the flower petals from the saffron crocus plant. Saffron is popular in nearby India, as well as in numerous other countries, as both a cooking spice and an agent for dyeing cloth. As many as 2,500 Afghan farmers grow the valuable saffron crocus.

raise horses, donkeys, and camels for transporting people and goods. Other animals exist in the wild. These include deer, foxes, wild goats, geese, and eagles. The eagle is particularly popular among Afghans. Many view it as their national bird, though the government has not yet made that choice official.

IN CASE YOU WERE WONDERING
Are native animals endangered, or at risk of dying out?
Yes. In 2009, the Afghan government issued its first-ever list of endangered animals, which can no longer be killed. Among them were wolves, snow leopards, Asiatic black bears, Pallas's cat, and the Laggar falcon. The US-based Wildlife Conservation Society helped the Afghans with the project. "This is an enormous step," says assistant director Peter Zahler. He thinks that Afghan communities "can and will take the steps to enforce these laws."[5]

A National Treasure and Hero of the Struggle

A few of Afghanistan's wild creatures live in the Kabul Zoo, built in the 1960s. During the decades that followed, enemy soldiers killed many of the zoo's animals. Even worse, some of these splendid creatures were cooked and eaten. Others died of starvation or neglect.

In recent years, the zoo has been making a bold comeback, says its director, Aziz Gul Saqeb. China, Pakistan, and other countries have donated new animals. The Chinese contribution consisted of two bears and two lions.

The lions were replacements for a male lion named Marjan. Germany gave him to the zoo in the late 1960s. Most Afghans came to see him as a sort of national treasure. But he became a symbol of the awful costs of almost constant war. In 1993, someone threw a grenade at Marjan. Although he survived, he lost one eye and all his teeth. He died of old age in 2002. "Look how he suffered,"[6] Saqeb says sadly, viewing an old photo of the scarred beast.

Such suffering is in the past, Saqeb adds, his mood brightening. Now, he explains, Marjan stands for the hope of a better future for Afghanistan, its animals and other natural wealth. To express that hope, a bronze statue of Marjan guards the zoo's front gate. Many Afghans see him as a hero—a symbol of Afghanistan's ongoing struggle for peace and prosperity.[7]

Marjan the lion, as he appeared before the awful injuries he suffered in 1993. After his death in 2002, the government had a bronze statue made of Marjan to symbolize hope for a better future for all Afghans.

This painting shows two Afghan tribal warriors as they appeared in the 1800s. The splendid costumes depicted here were not worn by average fighters. Only the leaders and a few other well-off members of a tribe could afford such expensive outfits and weapons.

CHAPTER 3
A Giant Battlefield

That events in modern Afghanistan are often disordered and violent, is not surprising. Most of the country's long history has been chaotic. The same thing can be said of the larger Middle East, of which Afghanistan is a part. For thousands of years, the region has been, in a very real sense, a giant battlefield.

The world's first empires arose in the Middle East. First came the Sumerians. They erected the world's first cities in southern Iraq at least 5,000 years ago. They fiercely fought one another for dominance.

Several more powerful conquerors and empire builders later sprang from that same region. Among them were Babylonians, Assyrians, and Persians. The warlike Assyrians reached their peak of power between 721 and 639 BCE. In the following century the Persians arose in southern Iran. Their armies swept outward, conquering neighboring areas. Sometime between 550 and 540 BCE, they subdued much of what is now Afghanistan. At its height in about 500 BCE, the Persian Empire was the biggest the world had yet seen. It covered the entire Middle East, except for southern Arabia.

Yet that mighty empire was not destined to last. It was regularly rocked by rebellions, which caused more disorder and misery. A great turning point came in 334 BCE. The Macedonian Greek king Alexander the Great invaded Persia and conquered it in only a few years. He absorbed much of Afghanistan into his new empire.

For a while after Alexander's death in 323 BCE, the Greeks ruled Afghanistan. But as the centuries wore on, one nation, people, or empire after another invaded it. Among them were Mauryans from India. In the 200s BCE, they introduced Buddhism to Afghanistan. Mauryan rulers also built large irrigation systems that made farming more productive. Later came the Kushans, from what is now southern China, and the Sassanians, from Iran. Each new realm held sway for a while. But sooner or later it grew weak and lost control.

A major **watershed** occurred in the early seventh century CE when Muhammad founded the religion of Islam in Arabia. Starting in 632, Arab armies spread outward from the Arabian Peninsula and assaulted the Sassanian realm. Within two decades Arabs ruled most of the Middle East. But it took them several more decades to achieve complete control of the tough, resistant Afghan tribes. The Arabs introduced their new faith to the Afghans, and it became the country's dominant religion.

For a couple of centuries, Arabs governed Afghanistan. But as time passed, still more foreign invaders swarmed across the Middle East. The strongest among them were the Mongols. Fearsome horse soldiers from central Asia, they overran Afghanistan in 1221.

Eventually, Mongol power weakened. As a result, in 1504 the Mughals, from northern India, seized several Afghan territories. But they and other foreign intruders were unable to

IN CASE YOU WERE WONDERING

What religions did Afghans follow before Islam was introduced?
Many Afghans adopted the faiths practiced by the foreign groups that ruled in Kabul and other large towns. This included the multiple gods worshiped by the Greeks who settled in Afghanistan following Alexander's conquest of Persia. Another example was Buddhism, introduced by the Indian Mauryans. Also, some Afghans became Hindus and Jews, a few of whom can still be found in the country.

overrun the whole country. Some parts remained in the hands of strong local tribes.

One of those tribes, the Pashtuns, established another milestone for Afghanistan. In the early 1700s, the tribe pushed the foreigners out of several Afghan areas. Then, in 1747 the foreigner then ruling Kabul was slain by his own bodyguards. The guards' commander, Ahmad Khan Durrani, was a Pashtun.

A forceful leader, Duranni soon united all the Afghan tribes. He ruled Afghanistan, which was finally an independent nation, as Ahmad **Shah** Durrani. Today Afghans recognize him as their country's founder. During his rule, he penned a poem about his beloved Afghanistan. "If the whole world be on one side and you on the other," he stated, "I'd much prefer your brown, arid plains. Ahmad Shah will never fail to hold you dear."[1]

The Afghans' troubles were far from over, however. In the 1800s and early 1900s, various parts of the Middle East again came under foreign control. This time, the intruders were powerful modern nations. Among them were Britain, France, and Russia. The British and French sought to dominate Iraq, Arabia, and several of their neighbors. At first, this was to give the two countries a military advantage in the region. Later, however, oil was found in huge quantities. France, Britain, and their allies used their military might to exploit that resource. Several Middle Eastern nations still resent this foreign meddling in their affairs.

Meanwhile, the British and Russians wanted to exploit Afghanistan. It lay in a strategic location—directly between Russia and British-controlled India. Control of Afghanistan would allow either Britain or Russia to keep the other from expanding in the area. Between 1839 and 1919, the British and Afghans fought three wars. Yet Britain was unable to gain any

This drawing was made by noted British surgeon, linguist, and artist James Atkinson (1780–1852) during the First Anglo-Afghan War, fought between 1838 and 1842. In the sketch, the British army enters one of the hundreds of rugged mountain passes that extend across much of Afghanistan.

lasting control of the stubborn Afghan tribes. After 1919, Afghanistan remained independent for several decades.

In the meantime, Russia had morphed into the communist-run Soviet Union. In 1978, some pro-Soviet Afghan leaders installed a communist government in Kabul. Other Afghans rebelled against the **regime**. So in 1979 the Soviets invaded the country to keep that government in power. For 10 bloody years the fighting raged on. An estimated one million Afghans died. But like so many other invaders over the centuries, the Soviets could not completely defeat the fearless, determined natives. So in 1989, they cut their losses and left.

The Soviets' exit did not bring stability to Afghanistan, however. The local tribes could not reach agreement and fought among themselves. In 1994, a group of extreme Islamic **fundamentalists** called the Taliban emerged and demanded peace. They told other Afghans that adopting their system would maintain peace. Many Afghans felt this approach might just work. By 1996, the Taliban had taken control of most of the country.

Most of those who had supported the new regime came to regret it. The Taliban kept order by shockingly brutal means. People who did not follow even minor rules were beaten or had hands or feet cut off. Some were publicly executed. The Taliban also prohibited the education of girls and closed down many schools.

Even worse, the regime allowed the Islamic terrorist group al-Qaeda (al-KYE-duh) to establish bases in Afghanistan. That group's leader, Osama bin Laden, ordered the devastating attacks of September 11, 2001. Members of al-Qaeda hijacked four US airliners. They flew three of them into buildings in New York City and Washington, DC, killing almost 3,000 people.

25

Responding to this outrage, the United States sent military forces to Afghanistan. They quickly toppled the Taliban, and with help from friendly Afghans drove al-Qaeda from the country. The Afghans set up a new, more democratic government. Protected by the Americans, they held open elections to choose new leaders. Most prominent among them was President Hamid Karzai.

Hammad Karzai, who became president of Afghanistan after the Taliban were defeated, gives a speech to some legislators in Kabul in January 2011. Karzai speaks fluent English without a trace of a Middle-Eastern accent.

Yet the Taliban steadily regrouped. They repeatedly launched attacks on both Americans and Afghans. As a result, US troops remained in the country for more than a decade. Most departed by 2014. But the Taliban still posed a serious threat. So, as had happened so often in the past, Afghanistan's future remained uncertain.

WIDELY VIEWED AS BARBARIC

The six years of Taliban rule proved hugely destructive for Afghanistan. Most of the outside world, along with many Afghans, came to see those religious extremists as barbaric. The Taliban did more than impose cruel, inhumane penalties for minor offenses. They also forced women into near-**servitude**. Girls could not go to school and women could not have jobs. Furthermore, women could not appear in public without covering their entire bodies, including their faces, with a cloth garment called a **burqa**.

Also, the Taliban destroyed thousands of priceless art treasures. They believed that looking at statues and other artifacts not created by Muslims was dangerous. It might lure Afghans away from Islam. In addition, sports and most forms of entertainment were forbidden. And it was not unusual for the Taliban's religious police to severely beat people for laughing in public.

According to Afghan-born American historian Shaista Wahab, the Taliban banned "playing or listening to music; dancing; television; makeup and nail polish; photographs of people and animals; flying kites; soccer; women leaving home without a male family member; male doctors treating women; education for girls (even in private homes); and women working outside the home." They also demanded "a dress code for men; a limited list of Muslim names that could legally be given to newborn children; separation of the sexes on public transport; and a minimum beard length for men."[2]

Members of a family of nomads gather outside their yurt. For many centuries, nomads in Afghanistan and other parts of southern and central Asia have lived in this portable dwelling. It consists of a number of wooden ribs bent down to form a circular skeleton that is then covered by large strips of felt (compressed wool) and/or animal hide.

CHAPTER 4
Diverse Peoples Seek Unity

Khadija Ghaznawi is one of a growing number of successful women business owners in Afghanistan. She also calls herself a peace activist. After decades of destructive wars, she says, the nation needs peace and prosperity. Like other well-educated Afghans, Ghaznawi recognizes that national unity is the principal key to that goal. "Achieving peace," she states, "is the main challenge that the people of Afghanistan must confront . . . peace will only be achieved through the unity of the men and women of Afghanistan."[1]

Ghaznawi realizes that achieving national unity will not be easy. Afghanistan has never been a strong, centralized nation. Rather, it has long been more of a loose collection of **ethnic** groups. Complicating matters, most of these groups are divided into smaller tribal units. For thousands of years, all these groups and tribes rarely got along. When they did, it was because they were all threatened by outsiders. Only during foreign invasions, says Shaista Wahab, did they "put their differences aside and unite against the common enemy."[2]

The members of the country's largest ethnic group are called Pashtuns. Their percentage of the overall population has varied over time. In 2014, it was about 42 percent. Most Pashtuns live in Afghanistan's southern region or in the capital, Kabul.

Mostly farmers, the Pashtuns strictly follow an unwritten code of honor called Pashtunwali. One of its main rules is to welcome anyone seeking help and offer aid to them. The code also calls for Pashtuns to seek justice or revenge when they are insulted or physically attacked.

The second-largest ethnic group is the Tajiks. Making up roughly 27 percent of the population, many of them live in the northeastern mountains. But Tajiks also make up a large proportion of the residents of Kabul and other **urban** centers. Because so many are urban dwellers, Tajiks have more government jobs than members of other ethnic groups. They also own numerous shops and other businesses in the cities.

The other Afghan ethnic factions are considerably smaller. The Hazaras, for instance, make up only around 9 percent of the population. They reside primarily in the central regions of the Hindu Kush range. Wahib points out that many Hazaras have "East Asian features," so they "may well be descendants of the Mongol invaders of the 13th and 14th centuries."[3]

Uzbeks also make up 9 percent of the population. They live mostly in the country's northern sector. The Aimaqs, at 4 percent, and Turkmen, at 3 percent, primarily inhabit the northwest.

Another factor that makes the Afghans diverse, as well as dividing them, is language. The country has two official languages—Dari, a Persian tongue, and Pashto, the traditional language of the Pashtuns. About 50 percent of the nation's

---

IN CASE YOU WERE WONDERING

How have the East Asian features displayed by many Hazaras affected the group's social standing over the years?

For a long time the group's members suffered from racial prejudice. Other Afghans viewed them as inferiors. As late as the 1800s, some were sold as slaves in Kabul. The Hazaras remained at the bottom of the social ladder in the 1900s. Finding it hard to find jobs in the countryside, many moved to Kabul in search of work. As a result, by the 1970s Hazaras—most of them poor—made up a third of the city's population.

inhabitants speak Dari, the language in which most Afghan literature is written. Speakers of Pashto make up around 35 percent of the population. Millions of Afghans are fluent in both. Some speak a third or even a fourth language. Often it is English. This is due partly to the presence of tens of thousands of US soldiers in the country between 2001 and 2014. In addition, at least 30 minor local languages are spoken in Afghanistan.

With their many languages and ethnic groups, it is hardly surprising that Afghans have been so divided for so long. Even today, differences of opinion can be sharp. And they sometimes lead to hurt feelings or angry outbursts. In December 2013, for example, General Abdul Wahid Taqat, a proud Pashtun, caused trouble when he went on a television talk show. "Pashtuns are the rulers and owners of Afghanistan!" he declared. "They are the real inhabitants of Afghanistan."[4]

These remarks insulted other ethnic groups. Heated protests erupted in both the media and in Kabul's streets. To restore calm, President Karzai, himself a Pashtun, had Taqat arrested. Karzai also made a speech that praised the virtues of national unity.

The president was aware that his countrymen had long shared one unifying cultural factor—religion. Nearly all Afghans are Muslims, the dominant religion in the country for many centuries. But by itself, that was not enough to maintain permanent unity. For the nation to prosper and endure, it was also necessary to have a strong central government.

Karzai was among the leaders who created Afghanistan's current democratic government. They pieced it together in the years immediately following the removal of the Taliban in 2001–2002. In some ways it resembles the US government. Both have an **executive branch**, headed by a president and vice president. One difference is that the Afghan version has two vice presidents instead of one. These individuals are elected directly by the people.

Also like the US, Afghanistan has a **legislative branch**. The Afghan version of the US Congress is the National Assembly. It has two houses. One is the 249-member House of People, and the other the 102-member House of Elders.

In addition, both governments feature a **judiciary branch** consisting of a Supreme Court and lower courts. In Afghanistan, the president appoints the high court's nine justices.

Still another similarity in the two systems is the way laws are enacted. A new law must be approved by both houses of the legislature. Then it must be signed by the president.

The new Afghan government is therefore structurally sound. But as late as 2014, it had not yet gained full control over all the country's peoples and tribes. Expert observers think this is partly because most Afghans are not yet used to national unity. Nor are they accustomed to modern democratic concepts and practices. It will likely take time for them to adapt to both.

In the meantime, farsighted Afghans like Khadija Ghaznawi continue to point the people in the right direction. They should "join their hands and work together," she says. It will require genuine trust and unity "to create a developed and free country where all people live in peace."[5]

IN CASE YOU WERE WONDERING

What is the term of office for the Afghan president and vice-presidents?
They serve for five years. They can run for re-election but cannot serve more than two terms.

WHO ARE THE NURISTANIS?

One of Afghanistan's most colorful ethnic groups is also its most mysterious. This is the Nuristanis, who dwell in the mountains northeast of Kabul. Their languages are unrelated to the others spoken in the country. Also, while they are Muslims today, their religious beliefs and customs were quite different from those of other Afghan groups before they converted in the late 1800s. Up until that point, they were known as "kafirs," or "unbelievers in Islam." Then they received the name "Nuristani," meaning "those who live in the land of the light."

Moreover, many Nuristanis have fair skin, red or blond hair, and blue eyes. In contrast, most other Afghans have darker skin, black hair, and brown eyes. During the late 1800s and early 1900s, scholars hotly debated the reasons for these physical differences.

One theory claimed that the Nuristanis are of Greek heritage. According to this view, they are descended from the Greek warriors Alexander the Great commanded when he invaded Afghanistan more than 2,300 years ago.

Over time, however, new evidence emerged that suggested another scenario. Most historians now think that the Nuristanis are descendants of an early people from southwestern Asia. Thousands of years ago, well before Alexander appeared on the scene, some members settled in what is now Afghanistan. The rest moved on and migrated into Europe.[6]

Two Nuristani farmers move their goats from one pasture to another. The origin of the Nuristatis remained a mystery until the late twentieth century.

These Afghan women have just completed a class in animal husbandry (the raising of animals for profit). Funded by the US government, the class is intended to teach Afghan women how to earn a living or at least to supplement their husbands' incomes.

CHAPTER 5
Families, Women, and Children

The family is the most important social unit in Afghan life. Family bonds are almost always strong. The average person has many of these bonds, because most families are extended. That is, they include aunts, uncles, cousins, and sometimes grandparents, as well as parents and children. With so many relatives close by, a growing child tends to feel safe. He or she also has many human resources from which to learn about life.

The vast majority of these families are **patriarchal**, or male-dominated, like the larger society. A tireless advocate of national unity, Khadija Ghaznawi also criticizes this time-honored male control of women. "The traditional patriarchal system," she explains, "takes root in the homes of Afghanistan and spreads up throughout the higher levels of society." Feeling oppressed by that system, she thinks it comes from "destructive, outdated customs."[1]

Ghaznawi dares to say publicly what many other Afghan women are afraid to. It is that women are often dominated by their fathers and husbands. That tends to keep women from reaching their full potential. Ghaznawi admits that treatment of women in the country has gotten better since the Taliban were ousted. "The improvements regarding women's legal status and rights in the past 10 years are positive developments,"[2] she says.

Yet Afghan women still lack certain basic freedoms and opportunities. As Trust in Education, an organization dedicated to improving the lives of Afghan women, points out, most marriages are **arranged**. A girl's father or other male relative chooses her husband. She has no say in the matter. Also, there has long been a family tradition of pushing girls into marriage when they are very young. "More than 50% of Afghan girls are married or engaged by [age] 10,"[3] the organization's website states.

Moreover, "most girls marry far older men—some in their 60s," it adds. Frequently, brides meet their husbands "for the first time at their wedding." A major reason for the continued practice of this custom is poverty. It "compels many parents to get their daughters married to avoid the cost of caring for them."[4]

Once they are married, teenage Afghan girls usually do not continue their educations. This is one of the primary reasons why a majority of female Afghans are illiterate.

People like Ghaznawi, who are dedicated to improving Afghan women's lives, see these customs as backward. Women "want to enjoy better opportunities for education and employment,"[5] she says.

Women's rights activists also want to see reforms in Afghan divorce customs and laws. At present, the father most often gets custody of any children in a divorce. Mothers naturally do not want to lose their children. As a result, few wives seek divorces, even if their husbands are abusing them.

Although many Afghan marriages are arranged, weddings are festive and happy events. They also tend to be expensive. Traditionally, the groom pays for everything, and often even poor young men go all-out. That means they must borrow the money, then pay it back a little at a time over several years.

In an online blog, an Afghan wife (who does not give her name) describes her wedding. She begins with the **nikkah**, or official marriage ceremony. It "takes place with the bride, groom, both sets of parents and close family members." Also present is "a religious Muslim authority," who performs the ceremony. "The bride wears a beautiful and modest green gown."

The ceremony is fairly simple, the wife continues. The holy man reads a passage or two from Islam's sacred book, the Quran. Next he recites "a special prayer" and "everyone congratulates the couple." The bride then "goes to change into her white wedding gown." In it she will "go to the reception where hundreds of people have come to celebrate."[6]

The young Afghan men shown here are dressed in formal modern-style suits because they are about to attend a friend's wedding reception. Some young adult Afghans have increasingly adopted Western clothing styles in recent years. White wedding dresses for brides is another example.

IN CASE YOU WERE WONDERING

What kinds of food are typically served at Afghan wedding receptions?
The Afghan national dish—*kabeli pilau*, consisting of meat and rice—is always on the menu. Other common foods served include lamb and chicken kabobs, various kinds of salads, and all sorts of vegetables. No reception would be complete without a variety of tasty pastries and other desserts.

At the reception, the guests welcome the bride and groom. Then the new couple "read the Quran together under a shawl" while everyone watches. After that, "the bride and groom are first to get food in a buffet style dinner." Finally, "there is the cake cutting and final goodbye to everyone."[7]

Afghan couples most often begin having children soon after they are married. Men usually hope for a boy. "Having a son in our culture is extremely important," the Afghan wife explains in her blog. With a son, "they can count on someone generating an income for their current and future financial needs." Also, "a son provides protection for the family."[8]

Afghan children enjoy playing, just as children in other countries do. But because they live in a war-torn land, they must be extra-careful *where* they play. Some parents do not allow their sons and daughters to play outside. Others allow it, but only in areas protected by guards. One such place is the Kabul Women's Garden. A pleasant park located in the capital, it has swings and places for kids to play ball. The park also has some small shops and eating places, says 13-year-old Zuhal. Sometimes she and her friends "look in the shops or buy a treat from the tea house."[9]

Growing numbers of Afghan children attend school. But there are still not enough classrooms to educate all the country's children. Plus, many families are dirt-poor. Instead of going to school, the children have to work to help out their parents. Yet

Several Afghan children and their parents enjoy a carnival ride at Qargha Lake, on Kabul's outskirts. The lake also features boating and swimming.

there is a thirst for education among the young. "There are so many girls who want to come to our school," says Shabona, who is 14. "We have to go to school in shifts so we can make room for the others."[10]

Whether attending school or not, most Afghan children envision a better future. Some girls dream they will one day achieve success or even fame. They know it can happen, thanks to Fawzia Koofi. She earned a seat in Afghanistan's National Assembly in 2005. She also campaigned for a while in the country's 2014 presidential election. Part of her success, she

Some of the schools in Afghanistan are religious in the sense that they focus on teaching children about the country's major faith. This student reads from Islam's most holy book, the Quran.

says, must be credited to her mother. As a child, little Fawzia heard her mother, Bibi, talking to a neighbor one day. "My daughter tries so hard," Bibi bragged. "I am sure she will become president!"[11]

IN CASE YOU WERE WONDERING

Why did Fawzia Koofi stop campaigning to become Afghanistan's president in 2014?
Government election officials disallowed her from running because of her age. By law, Afghans who run for president must be 40 years old. Koofi was only 39 at that time.[12]

BARTERED DAUGHTERS

All available evidence indicates that most Afghan fathers love their children, including their daughters. And they would not knowingly do anything that might harm them.

There are exceptions to the rule, however. Many of these exceptions are fathers who are strongly addicted to drugs, most often opium. That substance comes from poppies, flowers that grow in abundance in Afghanistan. There is a "skyrocketing addiction rate" for opium, says Afghan journalist Fariba Nawa. That rate is "more than one million in a nation of 30 million." The addiction often becomes overpowering, she writes.

To feed their drug habit, fathers borrow money from drug dealers and fall deeply in debt. Then, in desperation, they sell their daughters to pay what they owe. According to Nawa, "Thousands of young Afghan girls are being **bartered** into slavery." Typically, the dealers sell the girls to Afghan men who are looking for "second and third wives." Or they end up as the property of criminals who force them to work as prostitutes. Horrified, some of the girls kill themselves, Nawa points out. Others "run away and may end up in prison."

Over time, most come to accept their terrible fate. Nawa tracked down a girl named Darya, whose father sold her when she was 12. Now 22, Darya sadly told the journalist, "This was my destiny. I'm used to it now."[13]

Each year, thousands of young Afghan girls like this one are sold into slavery by their own fathers, usually because those men are addicted to drugs and desperate for money.

Shrouded by burqas, these Afghan women take part in a religious celebration. The Islamic religion, established in the 600s CE by the prophet Muhammad, is one of the main cornerstones of life and culture in Afghanistan.

CHAPTER 6
Religion as a Way of Life

"As you grow older, you will learn about loyalty," young Fawzia Koofi's mother told her. "You must be loyal to the true and good nature of your Islamic faith." It teaches that one has a duty to his or her family. Also, "be loyal to your friends." And "if they are true friends, then they will also be loyal to you."[1]

Through statements like these, as a child Koofi learned much about life. Many other young Afghans hear these same things from their parents. They learn that loyalty to family and friends is a bedrock value of Afghan society and life.

Yet Koofi's mother was careful to place loyalty to the Islamic faith before all other loyalties. This is because Afghans view their faith as a guiding force in everything they do. One scholar explains that in Afghanistan "religion is not an **ideology**," or a mere set of beliefs. Rather, it is a "way of life."[2]

Islam's influence on everyday life is visible everywhere in Afghanistan. It begins with its **constitution**, which went into effect in 2004. It states that citizens' civil rights and daily conduct all flow from their religious loyalty and duties.

For example, the constitution's opening sentence states clearly, "Afghanistan is an Islamic Republic." Its official faith "is the sacred religion of Islam." Moreover, "In Afghanistan, no law can be contrary to the beliefs and provisions of the sacred religion of Islam."[3] That is, the Afghans cannot make and enforce any law that goes against the basic teachings of Islam.

The first of those basic teachings is that only one god exists. Muslims call him **Allah**, while Christians and Jews call him by other names. A second central teaching is that Allah chose a series of **prophets**, or messengers. Among the most important were Abraham, Moses, and Jesus.

A third basic Islamic teaching deals with the final—and most important—prophet, Muhammad. Born in 570 CE, he was 40 when the angel Gabriel appeared to him. Gabriel imparted to Muhammad the text of Islam's sacred book, the Quran. Muslims, including those in Afghanistan, believe the Quran contains the rules that God wants people to live by.

One of these rules is called *salah*, meaning daily prayer. Five times a day, an Afghan prays to God. He or she kneels and faces southwest, the direction of the Arabian city of Mecca. It is where Muhammad was born. Each **mosque** has an official who reminds people when it is time to pray. In musical tones, he loudly calls out, "God is the most Great! I testify that there is no god but God. I testify that Muhammad is the Messenger of God. Come to prayer! Come to salvation! God is the most Great! There is no god but God!"[4]

Another religious rule is *zakat*, which is helping the poor in any possible way. Afghans are also expected to show respect to God by fasting during the month of Ramadan, the ninth month of the Muslim lunar calendar. During that month, Afghans fast from sunrise to sunset (Exceptions include children, sick people, and travelers). The three days following Ramadan are a celebration called Eid al-Fitr, which marks the end of the fast. Common customs during those three days are giving children gifts and serving guests tea, cookies, and candy.

IN CASE YOU WERE WONDERING

Do Afghans celebrate the New Year?
Yes. They call it Nawruz. They observe it on the first day of spring with feasting, dancing, singing, and playing games. Many people also plant new trees that day.

These Afghan Shia gather each year in July to celebrate the birthday of Muhammad al Mahdi, often called the Twelfth Imam. They believe that he was a twelfth-generation descendant of the prophet Mohammad.

Still another religious duty that Afghans perform is called the **Hajj**. If physically able, a Muslim is expected to journey to Mecca at least once in his or her life. Some Afghans make the trip several times.

In Afghanistan, and across the world, Muslims are divided into two groups: Sunnis and Shia (or Shiites). The split arose because Muhammad died without specifically choosing his successor. The majority of Muhammad's followers—the

Sunnis—chose Abu Bakr, his close friend and father-in-law, as the caliph, or leader. Others said that Ali, Muhammad's cousin and son-in-law, should have been selected instead. They became known as the Shia, a contraction of "shiiat Ali" ("supporters of Ali"). Years later, Ali did become caliph. But he was assassinated. Then Ali's son Hussein was killed in a battle with the Sunnis. As the respected magazine *The Economist* notes, "As time went on the religious beliefs of the two groups started to diverge."[5] At present, about 80 percent of Afghans are Sunnis, while the rest are Shia.

Many other common customs and practices in Afghan life have their basis in religious beliefs. Some are in a category widely seen as magical or superstitious by many foreigners. For instance, most Afghans view certain trees as sacred. To show respect, they tie pieces of cloth around those trees. They also pray at shrines dedicated to Islamic saints thought to have the power to cure illness.

Most Afghans believe in a harmful force called the evil eye. Supposedly it passes from one person to another through someone's gaze. In hopes of warding off this force, many Afghans wear magical charms. The most common one is the **hamsa**, an image of a two-thumbed hand with a blue eye in its palm.

IN CASE YOU WERE WONDERING

Is there bitterness or mistrust between Afghanistan's Sunnis and Shia? Sunnis and Shia throughout the Muslim world have long strongly disagreed with, and even hated, each other. In fact, bloody wars have been fought over their differences. In Afghanistan, the more numerous Sunnis traditionally look down on the Shia. It is not unusual for Shia Afghans to suffer from discrimination or even physical attacks.

THE FAMOUS BLUE MOSQUE

Afghanistan has numerous mosques and other religious shrines. One of the holiest and most beautiful is located in Mazar-i-sharif, in the northern part of the country. It is the Blue Mosque, erected in the 1100s. People gave it that name because its sides are covered with thousands of blue-colored tiles. Visitors come from across Afghanistan and numerous other nations to see the shrine. Its beauty is one obvious reason for its widespread popularity.

Many people also visit to pray at the tomb of Ali ibn Abu Talib, Muhammad's cousin and son-in-law who later became caliph. Many Muslims believe his body was moved from its original grave in Iraq following his assassination to the Blue Mosque long ago.

Both religious pilgrims and tourists remove their shoes at the front door. Before or after praying, many check out the mosque's small museum. They can also see the workshop of the special artisans who make the structure's replacement tiles. The chief tile-maker is Mohammad Shah. "I have been in the business for 24 years," he tells visitors. "Whenever there is something wrong with the tiles on the walls, or if some visitors pry off some tiles and take them away, we fix the damage."[6]

Shah and another expert tile-maker teach their craft to several apprentices. It is expected that someday they will have their own apprentices. That way, each new generation will have specially trained craftsmen to keep the mosque looking new.

This photo of one of the giant statues of Buddha created long ago in the cliffs near Bamiyan was taken shortly before the Taliban blew up these sacred relics.

Literature, Arts, and Entertainment

"I've been reborn amidst epics of resistance and courage," Afghan poet Meena Kamal wrote in her poem "I'll Never Return." She continues,

"I've learned the song of freedom in the last breaths, in the waves of blood and in victory
Oh, compatriot, oh brother, no longer regard me as weak and incapable
With all my strength, I'm with you on the path of my land's liberation."[1]

These stirring words are not just an example of emotionally moving poetry. When Meena composed them in 1981, soldiers from the Soviet Union were occupying her country. So the poem was partly a call to fight for freedom. Long before she was born, Afghans struggled to survive during wars. And poets through Afghanistan's history have penned similar calls to action in troubled times.

"Afghanistan has a rich literary tradition," says Monik Markus. Over the centuries, poems and other writings were penned by local Afghans. Others were produced by writers at "the royal courts of regional empires" that then controlled Afghanistan.[2]

In particular, Afghans in prior ages admired and promoted the works of Persian poets. This was partly because many Afghans spoke Dari, a version of Persian. Among the best of the pre-modern Afghan poets was Khushal Khan Khattak, a warlord from the Hindu Kush foothills who lived in the 1600s. His poems express the Pashtun social values he had learned as a child. An especially important one was maintaining family and tribal honor. "Life's no life when honor's left," he wrote. "Man's a man when honor's kept."[3]

Today's Afghan writers describe the forces that have shaped their lives. A well-known example is scholar and poet Latif Nazemi, who was born in 1947. Like many other Afghans, he was horrified by the Taliban's destruction of many national art treasures. Shortly after the Taliban were removed, he wrote "We Shall Return." In this poem, Nazemi promises that he and other writers who had fled the country "shall return to mourn the anniversary of the pillage of our books." And they will now "fill the hungry mouths" of the Taliban's guns "with dirt and gravel."[4]

Other arts, including sculpture and music, have long thrived in Afghanistan. Like native poets, Afghan sculptors often felt foreign influences. The aftermath of Buddhism's arrival in the area in the 200s BCE serves as an example. For several centuries, the faith prospered in Afghanistan. Local monks created numerous beautiful statues of Buddha, the revered founder of their religion.

The most famous examples are the Buddhas of Bamiyan. Created about 1,500 years ago in north-central Afghanistan, they were colossal. One stood 174 feet (53 meters) high, or 23 feet (7 meters) taller than the Statue of Liberty in New York Harbor. Outrage erupted across the globe when the Taliban blew up these cultural gems early in 2001. Today, many Afghans think the statues should be rebuilt.

Similarly, Afghan music has long felt the influences of the folk music of neighboring lands such as India and Iran. Afghans traditionally play folk music at a number of social events, such as New Year's celebrations and other holidays. Weddings also feature festive music. Wedding songs are frequently played by "a traveling people known as Jat, who are related to Gypsies," Markus explains. "They play their own variety of folk music."[5]

Most musical instruments in Afghanistan have counterparts in Western countries. They include local Afghan versions of the violin and flute. There are also cymbals and several types of drums. Particularly popular is a distant relative of the guitar, the **rubab**.

Singers often accompany musicians to produce traditional Afghan music. Much of it takes the form of love songs that two reporters call "haunting and beautiful, but unlikely to spice up a teenager's weekend."[6] For that reason, Western pop and rock music are slowly making their way into Afghan culture. Many younger Afghans welcome them. Among them is a high school student named Nasir. Members of his generation "are looking for something new and interesting," he says. "There is nothing we need in the old stuff."[7]

Nasir and other Afghans have more than music to entertain them. There are also sports and movies. Banned by the Taliban, they have been making a comeback in recent years. The national sport is *buzkashi*, which literally means "goat-grabbing." As Shaista Wahab explains, "it is a dangerous game" that had no rules until recent times. The players are "expert powerful horsemen." They "compete to grab and carry the headless carcass of a goat" from one point to another.[8]

The Afghans also play a wide variety of other sports. Soccer (known as football in Afghanistan) is perhaps the most popular. In 2013, the men's national team won its first major trophy, the South Asian Football Federation Championship. Six years earlier, the women's national team made its debut. Other common

IN CASE YOU WERE WONDERING

Did the national sport, buzkashi, originate in Afghanistan?
No. Historians believe the sport was introduced by the Mongols when they invaded in the 1200s.

sports include cricket, wrestling, boxing, archery, and martial arts. Rohullh Nikpai won the bronze medal in the martial art of taekwondo at the 2008 and 2012 Summer Olympics.

In 2008, two young Afghan men practice Taekwondo moves outside their home in Kabul. Several styles of martial arts are popular sports in the country.

Afghans thronged to movies throughout much of the twentieth century. But frequent wars destroyed many theaters. Then the Taliban outlawed movie-going altogether. Now films have returned, most of them made in India and Pakistan. Some theaters occasionally show American-made films.

Young Afghans are starting to make their own movies. Each year since 2004, some experienced British filmmakers have conducted workshops in Afghanistan. Students learn to shoot and show short films about their country. The program also has a larger purpose: doing whatever it can to help the Afghans heal, revive, and rebuild their war-torn nation.[9]

"I'LL NEVER RETURN"

Meena Keshwar Kamal was born in Kabul in 1956. As a young woman, she attended a local university. But eventually she quit, to devote more time to a cause close to her heart. It was a social movement that demanded more civil rights for women. When the Soviets invaded Afghanistan in 1979, Meena helped to organize anti-Soviet meetings. She also toured Europe, trying to drum up support for the Afghan freedom fighters.

These activities made her a target of the Soviets. The Afghan communist rulers they were supporting also wanted to eliminate her. Agents of those forces finally managed to kill her in 1987. Meena left behind several moving poems. Some, like "I'll Never Return," ably capture the spirit of the Afghan freedom fighters. The work states in part:

My nation's wrath has empowered me.
My ruined and burnt villages fill me with hatred against the enemy.
I'm the woman who has awoken,
I've found my path and will never return.
I've opened closed doors of ignorance. . . .
I've seen barefoot, wandering and homeless children. . . .
My voice has mingled with thousands of arisen women
My fists are clenched with the fists of thousands of compatriots.
Along with you I've stepped up to the path of my nation,
To break all these sufferings all these fetters of slavery. . . .
I've found my path and will never return.[10]

US Secretary of State Hillary Clinton poses with some leading Afghan women during one of her visits to Afghanistan. Afghan politician Fawzia Koofi, in the green headscarf, stands to Clinton's right.

KABELI PILAU

Kabeli Pilau is one of Afghanistan's most popular dishes. It is most often made with chicken or lamb. This is one of many recipes for chicken. It serves 5 to 6 people. IMPORTANT: The recipe calls for using hot stovetop burners and a hot oven. So make sure **an adult** is either aware you are making it or helps you make it.

Ingredients

2 cups basmati rice (although almost any rice will do)
2 to 2.5 pounds chicken, cut into bite-size pieces
3 cups chicken broth
2 medium onions or
   1 large one, chopped
½ cup golden raisins
1 cup fresh diced
   carrots (or carrot
   strips)
2 teaspoons cumin
1½ teaspoons
   cardamom
¼ tablespoon black
   pepper
½ cup vegetable oil
1 teaspoon butter
Pinch of salt

Instructions

1. Sauté the carrots and raisins in the butter and set aside.
2. Heat 2 tablespoons of oil and stir-fry the onions until they are soft. Then add rice and chicken broth, cover, and cook until the rice is soft but not quite fully cooked. Set aside.
3. Combine the cumin, pepper, cardamom, and salt and rub the mixture onto the chicken pieces. In a separate pan, pour in some oil and add the spice-covered chicken pieces. Fry for 5–6 minutes.
4. In a greased baking dish, place the chicken pieces in the center and cover them with the rice. Sprinkle carrots and raisins on top.
5. Put the baking dish in a preheated 325-degree oven and bake for 30–40 minutes.
6. Serve hot in a large flat dish.

PAPER HAMSA

The Hamsa is a Middle Eastern image or symbol intended to ward off evil, especially the widely feared "evil eye." For that reason, the Hamsa has a prominent "good eye" in the center. Traditionally, that eye is blue and rests on an upside-down hand with two thumbs. It is common to see various versions of the Hamsa in Afghan homes. Some take the form of necklaces, pendants, or other jewelry items. Others are plaques or even paintings done directly on walls. This paper Hamsa is frequently made by Afghan schoolchildren.

Materials

3 sheets of construction paper:
1 white, 1 pastel, 1 darker color
Pencil
Black pen or marker
Scissors
Light or medium-blue colored pencil
Paste or glue made for paper crafts

Instructions

Place one hand, with the fingers spread, on the pastel sheet. Using the pencil, trace its outline, except for the pinky finger. Remove the hand and place your other hand on the paper so that the fingers fit roughly into the outlines. Now trace your thumb, thereby creating the outline of a hand with 2 thumbs.

With the scissors, cut out the outline.

On the white paper, use the pencil to draw an oval lying on its side. Make each side of the oval come to a point. Inside the oval, draw another smaller version meant to represent an eye. Draw lashes on the upper and lower lines. Then draw a round pupil that touches the upper line. (You can use a coin to trace the pupil). Next, use the blue colored pencil to fill in the pupil. (Make sure to leave a small wedge of white uncolored, to represent the reflection of light on the pupil). Finally, carefully use the black pen or marker to darken the penciled lines.

Using the paste or glue, attach the cut-out hand to the darker sheet of paper, making sure that the hand is upside-down. When it is dry, glue the finished eye to the central part of the hand's palm. The completed paper Hamsa can be hung on a wall or door or pinned to a bulletin board. Or you can use a refrigerator magnet to attach it to the refrigerator or another

Official country name: Islamic Republic of Afghanistan

Official languages: Dari, Pashto

Capital: Kabul

Ethnic groups: Pashtun 42%, Tajik 27%, Hazara 9%, Uzbek 9%, Aimaq 4%, Turkmen 3%, Baloch 2%, other 4%

Religions: Sunni Muslims 80%, Shia Muslims 19%, other 1%

Area: 251,825 square miles (652,225 square kilometers), slightly smaller than Texas

Population: 31,800,000 (2014 estimate)

Largest cities: Kabul (3,100,000), Kandahar (515,000), Herat (398,000), Mazar-i-Sharif (375,000), Jalalabad (205,000)

Highest point: Mt. Nowshak, 24,557 feet (7,485 meters)

Lowest point: Amu Darya River, 846 feet (258 meters)

Longest river: Helmand River, 710 miles (1,150 km)

Average temperatures: Kabul: January 24°–42°F (-4°–6°C); July 66°–93°F (19°–34°C)

FLAG: The flag of Afghanistan was adopted by the Afghan Interim Administration on December 22, 2001. The flag consists of three stripes of the colors black, red, and green. The center emblem is the classical emblem of Afghanistan with a mosque with its mihrab facing Mecca.

TIMELINE

BCE

ca. 3000s	The cities of ancient Sumeria engage in rivalries and wars.
ca. 721–639	The warlike Assyrians reach their height of power and influence.
ca. 551–40	The Persians subdue what is now Afghanistan.
ca. 500	Under King Darius I, the Persian Empire reaches its furthest extent.
334	Macedonian Greek ruler Alexander III (later called "the Great") invades the Persian Empire.
330–27	Alexander conquers Afghanistan.

CE

651	Arab armies take control of most of the Middle East and spend several more decades seizing Afghanistan.
1220–1221	The Mongols invade Afghanistan.
1364	Asian conqueror Tamerlane conquers Afghanistan.
1504	The Mughals, from India, take control of Afghanistan.
1747	Ahmad Khan Durrani begins unifying the Afghan tribes and establishes the independent nation of Afghanistan.
1772	Durrani's son, Timur, begins ruling the country.
1839–1842	The Afghans fight the British in the First Anglo-Afghan War.
1878–1880	The two countries clash again in the Second Anglo-Afghan War.
1903	The Afghans establish their first secondary, or high, school.
1914–1918	As World War I rages, Afghanistan remains neutral.
1919	The Third Anglo-Afghan War is fought and Afghanistan emerges with its independence.
1927	The Afghans introduce their first uniform currency—the Afghani.
1940	A year after the start of World War II, Afghanistan announces its neutrality.
1946	Afghanistan joins the newly formed United Nations (UN).
1969–1972	A terrible famine kills about 100,000 Afghans.
1978	A communist regime comes to power in Afghanistan.
1979	To support the communist regime, the Soviet Union invades Afghanistan.
1989	The Soviets withdraw from Afghanistan.
1992–1994	Competing warlords struggle against one another for power in Afghanistan.
1996	The Taliban seize Kabul and take over the country.
2001	The terrorist group al-Qaeda, based in Afghanistan and protected by the Taliban, attacks the United States on September 11; the US strikes back and removes the Taliban from power.
2004	The reorganized nation of Afghanistan issues its new constitution.
2005	Fawzia Koozi becomes the first woman member of the Afghan National Assembly.
2014	The United States removes its combat units from Afghanistan.

CHAPTER NOTES

Introduction: They Will Bounce Back

1. Melody E. Chavis, *Meena, Heroine of Afghanistan* (New York: St. Martin's, 2010), p. 103.
2. Malalai Joya, *A Woman Among Warlords* (New York: Scribner's, 2009), p. 3.
3. Chavis, p. 103.

Chapter 1: A Day in Mustala's Life

1. Deborah Ellis, *Kids of Kabul* (Toronto: Groundwood, 2012), p. 46.
2. Ibid., p. 42.
3. Ibid., p. 46.
4. Ibid., p. 31.
5. Ibid., p. 45.
6. Ibid., p. 132.
7. Tony O'Brien and Mike Sullivan, *Afghan Dreams: Young Voices of Afghanistan* (New York: Bloomsbury, 2008), p. 47.
8. Ibid.
9. Ellis, *Kids of Kabul*, p. 47.
10. Ibid., pp. 46–47.
11. O'Brien and Sullivan, *Afghan Dreams*, p. 31.

Chapter 2: Natural Physical Features

1. Monik Markus, Embassy of Afghanistan in Washington, DC, "Afghanistan in Brief." http://www.embassyofafghanistan.org/page/afghanistan-in-brief
2. Shaista Wahab, *A Brief History of Afghanistan* (New York: Facts on File, 2007), p. 1.
3. Ibid.
4. Ibid., p. 9.
5. John R. Platt, "Afghanistan Names Its First Endangered Species." *Scientific American*, June 9, 2009. http://blogs.scientificamerican.com/extinction-countdown/2009/06/09/afghanistan-names-its-first-endangered-species/
6. Frederic Bobin, "Inside the Kabul Zoo: A Sign of Afghanistan's Future?" *Time*, July 4, 2011. http://content.time.com/time/world/article/0,8599,2080818,00.html
7. Ibid.

Chapter 3: A Giant Battlefield

1. A.R. Benawa, "Selections from Early and Contemporary Pashto Literature," *Pashto Quarterly*, vol. 5, Autumn 1981, p. 120.
2. Shaista Wahab, *A Brief History of Afghanistan* (New York: Facts on File, 2007), p. 218.

Chapter 4: Diverse Peoples Seek Unity

1. "Khadija Ghaznawi: The Key to Peace Lies Within Afghanistan," *Huffington Post: The Blog*, February 26, 2014. http://www.huffingtonpost.com/unveiling-afghanistan/khadija-ghaznawi-the-key_b_4858385.html
2. Shaista Wahab, *A Brief History of Afghanistan* (New York: Facts on File, 2007), p. 13.
3. Ibid., p. 16.
4. Azam Ahmed and Habib Zahor, "Afghan Ethnic Tensions Rise in Media and Politics." *New York Times*, February 19, 2014. http://www.nytimes.com/2014/02/19/world/asia/afghan-ethnic-tensions-rise-in-media-and-politics.html?_r=0
5. "Khadija Ghaznawi," *Huffington Post*.
6. Thomas Barfield, *Afghanistan: A Cultural and Political History* (Princeton, NJ: Princeton University Press, 2010), pp. 28–29.

Chapter 5: Families, Women, and Children

1. "Khadija Ghaznawi: The Key to Peace Lies Within Afghanistan," *Huffington Post: The Blog*, February 26, 2014. http://www.huffingtonpost.com/unveiling-afghanistan/khadija-ghaznawi-the-key_b_4858385.html
2. Ibid.
3. "Life as an Afghan Woman." Trust in Education, http://www.trustineducation.org/resources/life-as-an-afghan-woman/
4. Ibid.
5. "Khadija Ghaznawi," *Huffington Post*.

CHAPTER NOTES

6. "Afghan Weddings: What's the Cost? What's the Purpose?" Afghan Wife, October 2, 2012. http://afghanwife.blogspot.com/2012/10/afghan-weddings-whats-cost-whats-purpose.html

7. Ibid.

8. "Pregnancy in the Afghan Culture: First Comes Marriage, Then Comes the Baby!" Afghan Wife, May 11, 2012. http://afghanwife.blogspot.com/search/label/afghan%20baby%20boy

9. Deborah Ellis, *Kids of Kabul* (Toronto: Groundwood, 2012), p. 75.

10. Ibid., p. 58.

11. Fawzia Koofi, *The Favored Daughter: One Woman's Fight to Lead Afghanistan into the Future* (New York: Palgrave Macmillan, 2012), p. 98.

12. Sophie McBain, "Fawzia Koofi, the female politician who wants to lead Afghanistan." *New Statesman*, December 18, 2013. http://www.newstatesman.com/2013/12/just-ticket

13. Fariba Nawa, "In Afghanistan, Fathers Barter Daughters to Settle Drug Debts." *The Atlantic*, July 31, 2013. http://www.theatlantic.com/international/archive/2013/07/in-afghanistan-fathers-barter-daughters-to-settle-drug-debts/278217/

Chapter 6: Religion as a Way of Life

1. Fawzia Koofi, *The Favored Daughter: One Woman's Fight to Lead Afghanistan into the Future* (New York: Palgrave Macmillan, 2012), p. 69.

2. Thomas Barfield, *Afghanistan: A Cultural and Political History* (Princeton, NJ: Princeton University Press, 2010), p. 40.

3. "The Constitution of Afghanistan," Afghanistan Online. http://www.afghan-web.com/politics/current_constitution.html

4. Paul Lunde, *Islam: Faith, Culture, History* (New York: Dorling Kindersley, 2002), p. 19.

5. "The Economist explains: What is the difference between Sunni and Shia Muslims?" *The Economist*, May 28, 2013, http://www.economist.com/blogs/economist-explains/2013/05/economist-explains-19

6. Charles Recknagel, "The Timeless Beauty of Afghanistan's Blue Mosque." Radio Free Europe/Radio Liberty, May 25, 2011. http://www.rferl.org/content/timeless_beauty_afghanistan_blue_mosque/24204654.html

Chapter 7: Literature, Arts, and Entertainment

1. Meena Keshwar Kamal, "I'll Never Return." http://www.rawa.org/ill.htm

2. Monik Markus, Embassy of Afghanistan in Washington, DC, "Afghanistan in Brief: Arts and Culture." http://www.embassyofafghanistan.org/page/afghanistan-in-brief#4

3. Khushal Khan Khattak, "Life's No Life When Honor's Left." http://www.afghan-web.com/culture/poetry/pops/honorpoem.html

4. Sharif Faez, "Latif Nazemi: A Modern Afghan Poet and Critic." http://www.afghanasamai.com/Obaidi/safahat%20ekhtesasi/Latif%20Nazemi/latif%20nazemi.htm

5. Markus, "Afghanistan in Brief."

6. Jean MacKenzie and Mohammad Sediq Behnam, "Afghans, They're Just Like Us." *Global Post*, May 30, 2010. http://www.globalpost.com/dispatch/afghanistan/090729/the-musical-generation-gap

7. Ibid.

8. Shaista Wahab, *A Brief History of Afghanistan* (New York: Facts on File, 2007), p. 22.

9. "Arts in Afghanistan," British Council. http://www.britishcouncil.org/afghanistan-arts-arts-in-afghanistan.htm

10. Meena Keshwar Kamal, "I'll Never Return."

FURTHER READING

Books

Adams, Simon. *Afghanistan*. North Mankato, MN: Smart Apple Media, 2008.

Aslan, Reza. *No God but God: The Origins and Evolution of Islam*. New York: Ember, 2012.

Berlatsky, Moah. *Afghanistan*. San Diego: Greenhaven Press, 2010.

Bjorklund, Ruth. *Afghanistan*. New York: Children's Press, 2012.

Conover, Sarah. *Muhammad: The Story of a Prophet and Reformer*. Boston: Skinner House, 2013.

January, Brendon. *The Arab Conquests of the Middle East*. Minneapolis, MN: Twenty-First Century Books, 2009.

Nardo, Don. *The Birth of Islam*. Greensboro, NC: Morgan Reynolds, 2012.

Sheen, Barbara. *Foods of Afghanistan*. Farmington Hills, MI: Kidhaven Press, 2011.

Steele, Philip. *Afghanistan: From War to Peace?* London: Wayland, 2011.

Wittekind, Erika. *Afghanistan*. Minneapolis: ABDO, 2013.

On the Internet

"Afghanistan," National Geographic.
http://travel.nationalgeographic.com/travel/countries/afghanistan-guide/

"Biography of Hamid Karzai," Afghanistan Online.
http://www.afghan-web.com/bios/today/hkarzai.html

Works Consulted

"Afghanistan." CIA World Factbook. https://www.cia.gov/library/publications/the-world-factbook/geos/af.html

"Afghanistan." Earth's Endangered Creatures. http://earthsendangered.com/search-regions3.asp?search=1&sgroup=allgroups&ID=2

"Afghan Weddings: What's the Cost? What's the Purpose?" Afghan Wife, October 2, 2012. http://afghanwife.blogspot.com/2012/10/afghan-weddings-whats-cost-whats-purpose.html

Ahmed, Azam and Habib Zahor. "Afghan Ethnic Tensions Rise in Media and Politics." *New York Times*, February 18, 2014. http://www.nytimes.com/2014/02/19/world/asia/afghan-ethnic-tensions-rise-in-media-and-politics.html?_r=0

"Arts in Afghanistan." British Council. http://www.britishcouncil.org/afghanistan-arts-arts-in-afghanistan.htm

Barfield, Thomas. *Afghanistan: A Cultural and Political History*. Princeton, NJ: Princeton University Press, 2010.

Benawa, A.R. "Selections from Early and Contemporary Pashto Literature," *Pashto Quarterly*, vol. 5, Autumn 1981.

Bobin, Frederic. "Inside the Kabul Zoo: A Sign of Afghanistan's Future?" *Time*, July 4, 2011. http://content.time.com/time/world/article/0,8599,2080818,00.html

Chavis, Melody E. *Meena, Heroine of Afghanistan*. New York: St. Martin's, 2010.

"The Constitution of Afghanistan," Afghanistan Online.
http://www.afghan-web.com/politics/current_constitution.html

"The Economist explains: What is the difference between Sunni and Shia Muslims?" *The Economist*, May 28, 2013. http://www.economist.com/blogs/economist-explains/2013/05/economist-explains-19

Ellis, Deborah. *Kids of Kabul*. Toronto: Groundwood, 2012.

"The Evil Eye," *Knowledge Globe*, October 7, 2013. http://ato1952.wordpress.com/2013/10/07/the-evil-eye/

FURTHER READING

Faez, Sharif. "Latif Nazemi: A Modern Afghan Poet and Critic." http://www.afghanasamai.
    com/Obaidi/safahat%20ekhtesasi/Latif%20Nazemi/latif%20nazemi.htm

"The History of the Pashto Language," Afghan Network. http://www.afghan-network.net/
    Ethnic-Groups/pashtu-history.html

Joya, Malalai. *A Woman Among Warlords*. New York: Scribner's, 2009.

Kamal, Meena Keshwar. "I'll Never Return." http://www.rawa.org/ill.htm

"Khadija Ghaznawi: 'The Key to Peace Lies Within Afghanistan, Not Outside.'" *Huffington
    Post: The Blog*, February 26, 2014. http://www.huffingtonpost.com/unveiling-
    afghanistan/khadija-ghaznawi-the-key_b_4858385.html

Khattak , Khushal Khan. "Life's No Life When Honor's Left." http://www.afghan-web.com/
    culture/poetry/pops/honorpoem.html

Koofi, Fawzia. *The Favored Daughter: One Woman's Fight to Lead Afghanistan into the
    Future*. New York: Palgrave Macmillan, 2012.

"Life as an Afghan Woman." Trust in Education. http://www.trustineducation.org/
    resources/life-as-an-afghan-woman/

Lunde, Paul. *Islam: Faith, Culture, History*. New York: Dorling Kindersley, 2002.

MacKenzie, Jean and Mohammad Sediq Behnam. "Afghans, They're Just Like Us." *Global
    Post*, May 30, 2010. http://www.globalpost.com/dispatch/afghanistan/090729/
    the-musical-generation-gap

Markus, Monik. "Afghanistan in Brief." Embassy of Afghanistan in Washington, DC.
    http://www.embassyofafghanistan.org/page/afghanistan-in-brief

McBain, Sophie. "Fawzia Koofi, the Female Politician Who Wants to Lead Afghanistan."
    New Statesman, December 18, 2013. http://www.newstatesman.com/2013/12/
    just-ticket

Nawa, Fariba. "In Afghanistan, Fathers Barter Daughters to Settle Drug Debts." *The
    Atlantic*, July 31, 2013. http://www.theatlantic.com/international/archive/2013/07/
    in-afghanistan-fathers-barter-daughters-to-settle-drug-debts/278217/

O'Brien, Tony and Mike Sullivan. *Afghan Dreams: Young Voices of Afghanistan*. New
    York: Bloomsbury, 2008.

"Other Popular Sports Played in Afghanistan." Afghanistan Online.
    http://www.afghan-web.com/sports/spplayed.html

"Picture This: Capturing Afghanistan's Cinema Culture." Southern California Public
    Radio, December 4, 2013. http://www.scpr.org/programs/take-two/2013/12/04/34914/
    picture-this-capturing-afghanistans-cinema-culture/

Platt, John R. "Afghanistan Names Its First Endangered Species." *Scientific American*,
    June 9, 2009. http://blogs.scientificamerican.com/extinction-countdown/2009/06/09/
    afghanistan-names-its-first-endangered-species/

"Pregnancy in the Afghan Culture: First Comes Marriage, Then Comes the Baby."
    Afghan Wife, May 11, 2012. http://afghanwife.blogspot.com/search/label/
    afghan%20baby%20boy

Recknagel, Charles. "The Timeless Beauty of Afghanistan's Blue Mosque." Radio Free
    Europe/Radio Liberty, May 25, 2011. http://www.rferl.org/content/timeless_beauty_
    afghanistan_blue_mosque/24204654.html

Ruthven, Malise. *Islam: A Very Short Introduction*. New York: Oxford University Press,
    2012.

Tschannen, Rafiq A. "Buzkashi." *The Muslim Times*, March 6, 2014.
    http://www.themuslimtimes.org/2014/03/countries/afghanistan/who-is-the-grand-
    father-of-polo-answer-buzkashi-afghanistans-national-game

Wahab, Shaista. *A Brief History of Afghanistan*. New York: Facts on File, 2007.

GLOSSARY

adage (ADD-ij)—An old saying.

Allah (AH-la, or uh-LAH)—The name for God in the Islamic faith.

arranged marriage (uh-RAINJ'd MAIR-ij)—A union of a bride and groom that results from an agreement worked out by their fathers or some other male relatives.

backwater (BACK-wah-tuhr)—A backward place.

bartered (BAR-terd)—Sold or traded.

burqa (BUR-kuh)—A garment that covers a woman from head to toe, traditionally worn in a number of countries with large Muslim populations.

coed (COH-ed)—Featuring or involving both women and men.

constitution (con-stih-TOO-shun)—A written blueprint for a nation's government.

endangered (en-DAIN-jerd)—At risk of dying out or becoming extinct.

ethnic (ETH-nick)—Relating to a local people or culture.

executive branch (eg-ZEK-yoo-tiv BRAN'ch)—In a government, the president, vice-president and agencies responsible for daily operations.

fauna (FAW-nuh)—Animals.

fundamentalist (fun-duh-MEN-tuhl-ist)—A follower of rigid traditional rules and ideas, especially religious ones.

geography (gee-OGG-ruh-fee)—The natural physical features of a region, country, or continent.

Hajj (HAWJ)—A journey a Muslim takes to Mecca at least once in his or her lifetime.

hamsa (HAWM-zuh)—In Afghanistan and other Middle Eastern countries, a symbol or charm intended to ward off the evil eye.

ideology (eye-dee-AH-luh-gee)—A set of beliefs or principles.

illiterate (ill-IT-uhr-it)—Unable to read and write.

indigenous (in-DIJ-uh-niss)—Local or native to a particular place.

judicial branch (joo-DISH'l BRAN'ch)—The justices, or judges, who oversee a government's court system.

legislative branch (lej-uh-SLAI-tiv BRAN'ch)—The congress, national assembly, or other law-making body of a government.

mosque (MAHSK)—A Muslim place of worship.

mud-bricks (MUD-BRIK's)—Building materials made by packing mud or clay into wooden molds and leaving them out in the sun to dry.

nikkah (NEE-kah)—The official marriage ceremony in an Afghan wedding.

patriarchal (pat-ree-AR-kuhl)—Run or dominated by men.

populous (POP-yoo-lis)—Heavily populated, or packed with people.

prophet (PRAH-fit)—A person chosen by God to deliver messages to humans.

regime (ri-JEEM)—A government or group of rulers presently in power.

rubab (r'BAB)—A musical instrument somewhat like a guitar, but usually plucked, native to the Middle East and southwestern Asia.

salah (SAH-luh)—In Islam, praying to God each day.

servitude (SERV-uh-tood)—Slavery.

shah (SHAW)—A Persian word meaning "ruler," used as a title by leaders in some Middle Eastern countries.

strategic (struh-TEE-jik)—Important or opportune for a person or group.

urban (UHR-bin)—Having to do with cities.

watershed (WAH-tehr-shed)—An important moment or turning point.

zakat (z'KAHT)—In Islam, charity for the poor.

INDEX

Abu Bakr 46

Aimaqs 30

Alexander the Great 21, 22, 33

Ali ibn Abu Talib 46

Allah (God) 43

al-Qaeda 25, 26

Arabia 21, 22

Assyrians 21

Atkinson, James 24

Bamiyan 13, 48, 50

bin Laden, Osama 25

Blue Mosque 47

Britain/British 22, 24

Buddha/Buddhism 22, 48, 50

buzkashi (sport) 51

children 8–13, 38

Dari (language) 30–31, 49, 56

Darya (girl in slavery) 41

Dasht-i Margo desert 16

divorce 36

Durrani, Ahmad Shah 23

education 10–12

Egypt 6

Eid al-Fitr 44

endangered animals 18

English (language) 31

family 35–41

Gabriel (angel) 44

geography 14–18

Ghaznawi, Khadija 29, 32, 35

Greeks 21, 22, 33

Hajj (journey to Mecca) 45

hamsa 46, 55

Hazaras 30

Hindu Kush mountains 15, 30, 49

Hindus/Hinduism 22

Hussein (Ali's son) 46

India 20–23, 50, 52

Iran 9, 21, 50

Islam 22, 25, 31, 33, 37, 40, 42–43

Jeena (teenager in Kabul) 13

Jesus 22, 44

Joya, Malalai 7

Kabul (Afghanistan) 7–10, 12–13, 15–16, 22–23, 25, 29–31, 33, 38–39, 52–53, 56

Kabul Zoo 12, 19

Kamal, Meena Keshwar 6–7, 49, 53

Karima (girl in Kabul) 9

Karzai, Hamid 26, 31

Khattak, Khushal Khan 49

Koofi, Bibi 40, 43

Koofi, Fawzia 39–40, 43, 53

Kushans 22

Marjan (lion) 19

Markus, Monik 16, 49–50

Mauryans 22

Mecca (Saudi Arabia) 44, 56

Mongols 22, 30, 51

Mughals 22

Muhammad 22, 42, 44–46

Mustala (boy in Kabul) 9–10, 12–13

National Assembly (of Afghanistan) 32

Nawa, Fariba 41

Nazemi, Latif 50

New York City 25

nikkah (marriage ceremony) 36

Nuristanis 33

oil 23

opium 41

Pakistan 14, 19, 52

Pashto (language) 17, 30–31, 56

Pashtuns 23, 29–30, 49, 56

Pashtunwali 29

Persia/Persians 21–22, 30, 49

Qargha Lake (Kabul) 39

Quran 37–38, 40, 44

Ramadan 44

religion 22, 42–48

Rhamat (boy in Kabul) 11–12

rubab (guitar) 51

Russia 23, 25

saffron 18

salah (prayer) 44

Saqel, Azziz Gul 19

Shabona (teenager in Kabul) 39

Shia 45, 56

Sigrullah (girl in Kabul) 10

Soviets/Soviet Union 25, 49, 53

Sumerians 21

Sunnis 45, 56

Tajiks 30

Taliban 25–27, 31, 35, 48, 50–52

Tarzi, Mahmud 15

Turkmen 30

United States 18, 25–26, 31–32, 34

Uzbeks 30

Wahab, Shaista 16–17, 27, 29–30, 51

weddings 35–38, 50

women 25, 27, 34–43

zakat (charity) 44

Zuhal (girl in Kabul) 38

About the Author

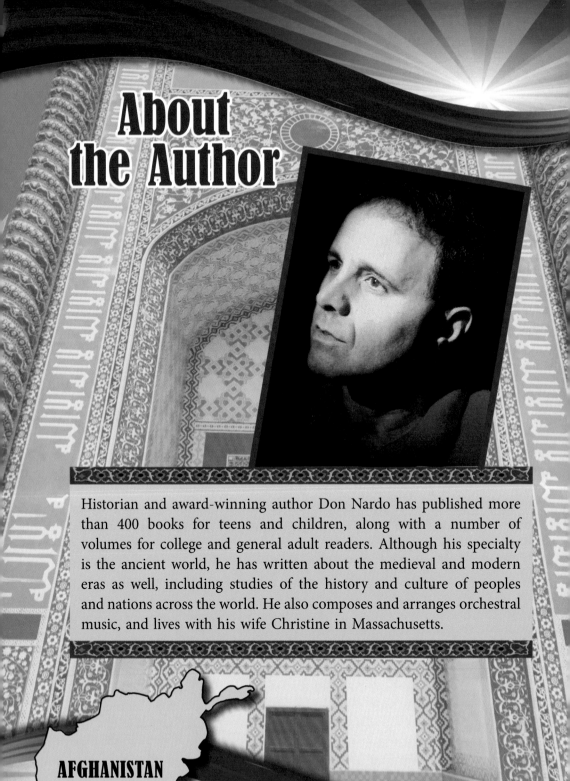

Historian and award-winning author Don Nardo has published more than 400 books for teens and children, along with a number of volumes for college and general adult readers. Although his specialty is the ancient world, he has written about the medieval and modern eras as well, including studies of the history and culture of peoples and nations across the world. He also composes and arranges orchestral music, and lives with his wife Christine in Massachusetts.

AFGHANISTAN